Faithful Voices

Oral Readings
Exploring Beliefs in Action

To the Friends at
West Falmouth Meeting

Faithful Voices

Oral Readings
Exploring Beliefs in Action

by Ed Schwartz

Quaker Press
of Friends General Conference
Philadelphia, Pennsylvania

ISBN-10: 1-888305-40-1
ISBN-13: 978-1-888305-40-1

Library of Congress Cataloging-in-Publication Data
Schwartz, Ed (Ed M.), 1938–
    Faithful voices : oral readings, exploring beliefs in action / by Ed Schwartz.
       p. cm.
    ISBN-13: 978-1-888305-40-1
       1. Christian life—Quaker authors.   2. Monologues, American.   I. Title.
    BX7738.S39   2005
    289.6—dc22   2005028980

Book design and composition by David Budmen

Front cover illustrations:

First row (left to right): Swarthmoor Hall—home of Margaret Fell and center of early Quakerism, George Fox and John Woolman

Second row: Rufus Jones

Third row (left to right): Faye Honey Knopp, Myles Horton, Dorothy Day and Emma Goldman

Fourth row (left to right): Dr. Martin Luther King, Jr., Juanita Nelson and Ed Nagel

For further information about this publication
and other Quaker resources, please contact:

Friends General Conference
1216 Arch Street, 2B
Philadelphia, PA 19107
215-561-1700
Or find us at www.quaker.org/fgc

To order this or other publications call 800-966-4556,
e-mail bookstore@fgc.quaker.org or you can order from us on the web at
www.quakerbooks.org.

Contents

Preface

Each of the "faithful voices" included in this volume could be regarded as a failure. Whether their "outreach" (their social activism) was guided by a formal philosophy (religious, social, political), or by a more amorphous declaration of "love" and "personal integrity," each could be perceived as working toward goals that were never (and perhaps, never could be) fully realized.

And so what was really gained?

Nothing seemed to cohere. Each "advance" seemed to precipitate a calamitous backlash and/or a dilution of an original goal. So few others seemed to understand the "stakes." The bulk of society often showing itself indifferent (if not merciless) toward their efforts. And of course each activist carried the weight of his or her own personal anguish—death, illness, the separation from family and friends. Sometimes incarceration came into play—and sometimes poverty.

Were their struggles worth it? Would they again pick up the "cross?" And what is their legacy?

Where is the return to the "primitive Christianity" envisioned by George Fox and Margaret Fell?

Has John Woolman's sense of compassion really spread?

What of the anarchist dreams of Emma Goldman?

And the Catholic Worker communes of Dorothy Day?

Would Fay Honey Knopp appreciate the current state of sex offender treatment?

Did Dr. Martin Luther King, Jr.'s Civil Rights movement really advance beyond its Southern "Christian" beginnings?

Can the sweet mysticism of Rufus Jones still be sustained?

And what about Juanita Nelson's individual sense of nonviolent dissent?

How fares the "free school movement" envisioned by Ed Nagel?

And what is the state of Myles Horton's Highlander Folk School—that crucible for radical democracy?

Has time passed these visionaries by? Would they have considered *themselves* failures? Were their struggles worth the commitment of time and personal heartache? Did society's persistent opposition surprise them?

And how would they have defined success? Were the fruits of victory (the stated goals of their specific historical struggles) their only concern? Or had they a sense of something greater? Were all of them in a sense spiritual—if not religious? And what is the link between their spirituality and their acting in the world?

And are these questions only for them? For we too have felt the desire to act. And we too have witnessed its inherent frustrations.

How does one sustain these struggles that often seem hopeless? How does one move continuously uphill?

Wouldn't it be better to retreat (we sometimes argue) to circumscribe one's goals—to live more sanely? We should concentrate more on family and friends—on smaller acts of kindness.

Why not consider *gentle* reform? Must society always be the enemy, the adversary? Aren't we in debt to our society, our country, our culture? Doesn't it provide us with context—with definition and choice? It is the only world we know. It is the ocean where we swim. Why not (for the most part) accept its explanations, its basic premises? Life is short. We are merely human. We cannot move mountains.

But yet . . . ?

Faithful Voices: Oral Readings Exploring Beliefs in Action is comprised of scripts for oral (group) reading, and queries for group discussion. In writing these scripts (each of them based on persons who persistently lived their beliefs) the author has employed the following techniques: First, to explore examples of something his subject has written or spoken. Then, to put this material aside, giving it a chance to simmer, to merge with his own personality. Finally to create a script that for him "speaks" for that person. Such a script might take the form of a journal, a speech, a personal narrative, or even a fanciful story that seems to exemplify his subject. And it is important that these scripts be musical, poetic— that they can be read and listened to with enjoyment.

All of these scripts, then, are artworks. They are in the writer's own voice. And they are joined to queries constructed not to provide direct answers, but to probe more deeply into the questions themselves—into the dialogue between belief and action.

Facilitator's Guide

These scripts (written to be read aloud) explore the tensions between spirituality and acting in the world.

They are short choral dramas inspired by the lives and writings of such profound spiritual leaders such as John Woolman, Margaret Fell, George Fox, Dorothy Day and Dr. Martin Luther King, Jr.

The readings are accompanied by queries (questions for discussion) designed to be considered in the Quaker process of worship-sharing.

Here is a way to begin: Half the group are given a script to read. Those listening become an audience for those reading. In the second reading, the two sides exchange parts.

The story is heard at least twice. No other preparation is necessary.

The reading is simple, and the effect immediate. The texts are designed to have a musical, poetic sound. Each reader takes a line (no matter how short) and then passes on to the next reader—and so on. This process continues until the story is done. There should be at least three readers with no *upper* limit. The scripts can be used in any order, using as many or as few as needed. Also, they can be arranged in any combination, for example: just the women, only the Quakers, or the most modern "voices."

The process is both participatory and artistic. The readings contain both the tension of drama and the rhythmic consideration of poetry.

After the readings, the group is ready for the queries. The facilitator can choose a query or queries that she/he feels most relevant. The group goes into a silence, a worship-sharing mode. The participants only speak when moved. Whatever is prompted by the query is acceptable. There is neither debate nor discussion nor argument. The responses are like stones being dropped in a pond—with the circles given a chance to widen. In this way the query is not answered but deepened, the questions leading to other questions.

Quakers use worship sharing as a means to a deep discussion. But other methods and techniques can be employed such as gentle, orderly conversations with each participant having a chance to speak once before others repeat.

Margaret Fell

Swarthmoor Hall, home of Margaret Fell and the center of early Quakerism.

Margaret Fell (1614–1702), the "mother of Quakerism," the wife of George Fox, was often punished for her beliefs. Along with many other Quakers she suffered the cruelty of imprisonment and the possible loss of property. But her faith in God never wavered. The experience of Jesus (suffering leading to salvation) was her model. And her own troubles never kept her from reassuring others.

Margaret Fell Reading
(on hearing of her grandchild's illness)

My dearest

dearest John

try not . . . "my sweet"

(my dearest son-in-law)

no

to be so unhappy

(so terribly . . . distraught).

Because I know

(my dear)
that there is always . . . "something"
there is always some . . . "terrible catastrophe"
that plagues us
and pursues us
and presses so . . . fitfully
against our lives.

And at these "moments" . . . my darling
(at these hazardous times)
we would gladly . . .
(I know)
die ourselves
slip unseen
into some vast . . . and final darkness.

But there . . . my darling
(there . . . I tell you)
in that deep despondency
(in that dark despair)
our sweet Redeemer
(our Good Lord . . . Jesus Christ)
stands waiting . . . my darling

and leads us . . . not
(no)
toward some . . . "perfect paradise"
(toward some . . . "golden shore")
but away . . .
(away)
. . . from such "notions"
(from such . . . "sweet escapes").
And asks us then . . . my darling
simply . . .
(yes)
. . . to love Him
(to adore Him)
to bear . . . once more
His bloodied cross.

O John
(my John)
(my dear sweet long-suffering John)
if she dies . . . our "baby"
(if she "passes" . . . our precious child)
the Good Lord
(yes)

will reclaim her . . . I know.
The Good Lord
(yes)
will hold her
(and caress her)
and carry her home.

(and she will be happy there)

(and she will be safe)

For God is our refuge . . . my darling.

For God . . . is our resolve.

("O surround us . . . O Lord!
O contain us completely!
Then through all . . . fire
we are able to pass!")

O my darling!
My dearest dear!
Our hearts may shatter.
Our footsteps strain.

We grovel.
(we groan)

We stumble.
(we fall)

Nothing seems certain.
Nothing seems true.

We are pierced.
(we are stricken)

We are battered.
(we are maimed)

We cry "Jesus!
O Jesus!
O Glorious . . . merciful
Compassionate Jesus!"

And we are lifted . . . my darling!
(we are raised)
We are enveloped!
(we are held)

For we are his lambs . . . my darling.

(We are his own)

We are walking toward Calvary.

We are privileged to live!

Margaret Fell Queries

1. Margaret Fell advises her son-in-law that Jesus becomes available at our most despairing moments.

   Why doesn't Jesus *prevent* these moments? Why does he not *immediately* rescue us, leading us toward some perfect paradise?

2. Margaret Fell asks John simply to *love* Jesus. This, she says, will make John able to bear his own "bloodied cross."

   Is simply "loving Jesus" enough? Isn't the Bible full of rules and commandments?

3. And why, at the *peak* of our suffering, does Margaret Fell say that we will be "lifted," "raised," "held" and "secured?"

   Is suffering the only way to salvation?

4. Why does Margaret Fell, after so much hardship and persecution, conclude "that we are privileged to live?"

5. Will Margaret Fell's son-in-law be helped by this letter?

George Fox

George Fox (1624–1691) was the founder of Quakerism, and its greatest apostle. But right from the beginning the Quakers faced fierce and persistent persecution, especially from the Puritan ruler, Oliver Cromwell. Cromwell was Fox's greatest antagonist, although they met only three times during the former's short reign.

George Fox Reading

And so
I was taken ... forthwith
to Whitehall
to Oliver Cromwell
(to the protector himself).
And he asked me ... if I
(or any of my faction)
had been plotting in secret ...
... against his rule.

But I answered him ... that no
(no)
we *had* not
nor *would* not ... ever

(no)
lift a sword
against any man.

And he seemed
(then)
reassured . . . did Cromwell
and bid me take
some comfort there.

"But no
(no)
I could not stay!"
(I answered him.)
"That leisure . . .
(no)
. . . was not my intention!"
But peace . . . I wished for his house
and the true knowledge
of the living Christ.

And we agreed . . . then
to part.

But at James Park riding . . .
 . . . again I saw him
this peacock

(this arrogant man)
in his fine coach . . .
. . . and regal trappings.

And I called out to him . . . "Beware poor man!
Protect your soul!
Lay down your cross . . .
. . . at the feet of Jesus!"

And he stiffened . . . at my pronouncement.
And cried out to me . . . "Come closer!
Come closer to me George Fox!"

But so hideous
he had become
(this oppressor)
this ravager . . .
. . . of our Society.
So many Quakers . . . had he jailed
(so many)
that I cried out to him . . . "Repent!
(repent!)
Repent . . . poor sad
and sorrowful man.
For it's Christ Jesus . . .
. . . that you shunneth!

Look to your salvation!

Take heed!

Fear greatly . . .
. . . the living God!"

And for one last time . . .
(alas)
. . . did I see him passing
(this scourge)
(this tormentor of our people).
But pitiful . . . he now seemed
(distraught).
By a "darkness" . . . he was covered
(by a "gloom").

And I said to myself:
"Here indeed . . . is a desolate man!
Here indeed . . .
. . . is a living corpse!"

And soon after . . .
(we were told)
. . . some guardsmen came
(some soldiers . . . faithful
to the returning king)

George Fox

And they captured him . . . this tyrant.
And led him . . . to a hanging place
to a gallows . . . built
on a dismal hill.

And there
(there)
without pause
(without ceremony)
bound up his arms
and haltered his neck.
And cursed him
(and abused him)
and lifted him . . . weeping
high up in the air.

And so doth the Lord . . .
. . . repay the oppressor.
And so doth the Lord . . .
. . . go striking him down.

(smiting him)
(destroying him)

His own foul deeds . . .
. . . insuring his fall.

George Fox Queries

George Fox tells Oliver Cromwell that the Quakers would not "lift a sword against any man."

But when Cromwell ignores Fox's warning to "repent," and continues in his persecutions, Fox gets increasingly angry.

He seems to "give up" on Cromwell. And even envisions him as a "dead man"—as a "living corpse." And when Cromwell is executed by the state, Fox proclaims: "And so doth the Lord repay the oppressor . . . His own foul deeds insuring his fall."

1. When offered, should George Fox have taken "hospitality" at the home of Oliver Cromwell, in search of that "light of God in every man?" Or would socializing with Cromwell have blunted his opposition to Cromwell's cruelty?

2. Fox cries out to Cromwell to "Repent!" and "Beware!" in the style of an Old Testament prophet.

   Would Quakers today feel comfortable with such direct expressions?

   Do Quakers today feel less of a sense of political urgency? Of sin?

   Has Quakerism become too "subtle," too "moderate?"

Are Quakers today less willing to "speak truth to power?"

3. By not condemning the state's execution of Cromwell, is Fox being a hypocrite? Is he betraying his Quaker/pacifist principles: "we will lift no sword against any man"?

Fox feels that Cromwell's own foul actions insured his "fall." But when the state wielded its sword, should Fox, in spite of his feelings toward Cromwell, been opposing this act, this sentence of capital punishment?

4. Fox often refers directly to Jesus. Why do you think this makes some Quakers feel uncomfortable?

John Woolman

John Woolman (1720–1772) was the
tenderest of Quakers. He felt the pain of
the Negro slaves and the persecuted
Indians. But he felt, in true Quaker
fashion, that the light of God exists in all
persons. And so even the slave-holders he treated with
respect, hoping to achieve more through friendly dialogue
than by accusation. His journals, in their quiet way, reflect
his vision and bravery.

John Woolman Reading

And we took
then
(Josiah and I)
Randall's small boat
directly down-river
(to the fork at North Farrington)
meeting there
(praise God)
with Robert Calvert
and his wife ... Mary Calvert.

(and her cousin Thomas Dobbs)

Stopping there immediately
to pray
 and to thank our Lord
(our God)
for this convening.

And proceeded then
(directly)
to the large farm
owned by George Lenox.

Where we found
(stooping)
at brute . . .
. . . and demeaning labor
many somber Negroes
(field slaves)
bent women . . .
. . . and ragged children.

And decided . . . then
(in this circumstance)
to take neither rest

(nor nourishment)
at this location.

(at this place of slavery)

And George Lenox . . .
(the land owner)
. . . came out to us
and offered us . . . then
warm food . . . and cooling drink.

(bidding us to stop there)

But we balked . . . greatly
(at this request)
and said
that no . . . no
we could not
(no)
so easily do so
because of this slave keeping.

(so vile to us)

And he displayed . . . then

much uneasiness
(did George Lenox)
and raised up . . .
(high)
. . . his hand
and swore . . .
(yes)
. . . that only out of duty
(out of necessity)
had he held those Negroes captive.

(as a boon . . .
he said
. . . to his growing family)

And Mary Calvert . . .
(and her cousin . . . Thomas Dobbs)
. . . accepted these words,
and agreed that we might indeed . . .
(yes)
. . . take comfort there.

("to forgive as the Lord forgives")

(and Josiah Randall agreed)

But the hand . . .

(the fire)

. . . of our loving God

(his sweet insistence)

(yes)

fell hard upon me.

(and to the ground . . . I fell)

And I cried out

(with great anguish)

that never . . .

(never)

would I drink the blood

(no)

of these Negro children.

Nor eat . . .

. . . of their precious flesh.

(these words pouring forth from me)

(and I sat there quietly)

(and the others joined me)

And George Lenox

(much astonished)

admitted . . . then

that this slave-keeping

(this abomination)

had long . . .

(long)

. . . been disturbing his dreams.

(these dark faces . . .

. . . haunting him nightly)

And then he walked with us . . .

(then)

. . . back to the river

(did George Lenox).

And the Calverts

(with tender affection)

embraced him

and made leave to depart.

(as did their cousin Thomas Dobbs)

And Josiah Randall

(also)

began his preparations

twisting

and turning . . . his small boat.

(which I promptly boarded)

And George Lenox . . . then

(standing alone)

removed . . . sweetly

his hat

and waved it . . . vigorously

and shouted . . . "Farewell!

Farewell good friends!

Farewell!"

(his aspect glowing)

(these events taking place . . . in the month of June

in the year of our Lord

seventeen-sixty-three)

John Woolman Queries

1. George Lenox argues that he kept slaves "only out of necessity." That he does have a large family to maintain, and so needs the labor of slaves.

   Is Lenox being unreasonable? Isn't it a father's duty to care for his family?

2. Mary Calvert is ready to accept the hospitality of George Lenox (a slave-holder). She argues that we must "forgive as the Lord forgives." That Jesus himself advocated the forgiveness of sins.

   Isn't Mary Calvert being truly "Christian?"

3. John Woolman falls to the ground, and then declares that he would never "drink the blood of these Negro children, nor eat of their precious flesh."

   Is this behavior "Christian?"

4. In response to John Woolman the others sit also. And George Lenox suddenly reveals his own uncertainty about slave-keeping.

   Can you explain this dramatic turnaround?

5. As John Woolman and his friends are leaving, George Lenox, with great exuberance, waves goodbye.

   Do you think he will continue to keep slaves? Why? Why not?

Rufus Jones

Rufus Jones (1863–1948) traveled all over the world teaching, writing books and leading the American Friends Service Committee. But the sweet mysticism of his Quaker upbringing never left him. Always he reflected the sanctity and devotion of his home life—the farms, the hills and the forests of rural Maine.

Rufus Jones Reading: A Christmas Story

It was Christmas
(in the year 1872)

And the snow was falling.

And the tree
(the little Christmas tree)
delighted . . . the boy
with its perfect candles
(and tiny beads).

But something . . .
O!

(something)
yes
. . . was terribly wrong.

And his aunt
(his sweet
and gracious
"Auntie Peace")
kissed him . . . she did.
And hung up . . .
. . . the little cloth angel.

("Teresa" . . . he called it)

And she told him . . .
(then)
. . . that something bad had happened.
(something awful)

That his dog . . .
(his faithful companion)
(his sweet
and wonderful "Patch")
. . . had disappeared that night.

That his little . . . bed
was standing empty.

That he was . . . nowhere
to be seen.

"His tracks" . . .
(she said)
. . . "led straight to the hen house.
But then they stopped there.
(they disappeared)

It was like . . . the earth
had swallowed them."

And the little boy
(then)
grew so frightened . . . he did.
(grew so afraid)
For he loved . . .
(and cherished)
. . . his faithful friend.

And he peeked out . . .
. . . of their little window.
(into the whiteness)

(onto . . . the flat
and barren fields)

And a dot . . .
. . . he looked for.
A little dot . . .
. . . that would become his Patch.

But everything . . . was silent now.
(everything . . . was still)

And his father . . . then
came walking in.
And he hugged . . .
. . . his small son.
(and kissed him)
And told . . . the boy
that the worst
had happened.

(that something . . . terrible
had occurred)

That some hair . . . was found
down by the wood-pile.

(and some slaver)

(and some blood-spots . . .
. . . dotting the snow)

O Patch!

And they all joined hands
in a tiny circle
(the boy, his aunt . . .
. . . and his gentle father).

And the boy trembled.

And never . . . before
had he felt so sad.

But then
(just then)
the door
of their little . . . house
came swinging open.
And Joe came in.
(Joe Aaronson)

And he was carrying . . .
. . . in his arms
something limp.
(something drooping)

And it was Patch!
It was Patch . . . he was carrying!

And his father . . . cried
"Joe!
Joe!
Is that our Patch?
Is that our darling dog?

It looks like . . .
. . . the wolves got at him."

And Joe agreed.
And said . . . that he found him lying
down by the crossroads.
That he was left out there.

(that he was barely alive)

And then they . . . all
(the four of them)
knelt over his body.
(and the boy . . . felt
that he too
had been pierced)

And his father prayed:
"The Lord is my shepherd
(I shall not want).

He maketh me . . .
. . . to lie down in green pastures.

He leadeth me . . .
. . . beside the still waters.

He restoreth my soul."

And the boy . . .
(then)
. . . kissed his best friend.
(and caressed him)

And the wind blew.

And the snow kept falling.

And nothing mattered . . .
(now)
. . . except their dog.
(their fallen comrade)

His stirring.
(his breathing)

His sweet . . .
. . . and pulsing life.

Rufus Jones Queries

Rufus Jones saw the great story of Jesus of Nazareth as a continuing drama, one that is perpetually reoccurring—infusing life with majesty and meaning.

1. Can you identify events in your own life that infused events seemingly ordinary and natural that provided a glimpse into something greater?

2. Does the Christmas season seem to you a sacred time? Or the opposite, an irritant—a time of unbridled commercialism? And can these two states occur simultaneously?

3. Have you ever had a blinding moment—a brief insightful flash that made you feel connected to the "very source of life"—an experience that has never completely disappeared?

4. Is the feeling of sacredness more available *away* from urban centers? Is the experience of God more possible in rural areas, in nature itself? Is transcendent meaning (an intuition of God) a casualty of modern times?

5. Can the calamitous illness/injury (or even death) of a loved one contain a positive side—a sense of exhilaration, a feeling of life being lived at the core?

6. Rufus Jones traveled all over the world and had many accomplishments. But is social political activism risky? Can it move one away from one's spiritual center?

Emma Goldman

Emma Goldman (1869–1940) came to the
United States from Russia at the age of
seventeen. She was above all an anarchist—a
believer of people joining together to act
directly on their own behalf. And to make
rules only when needed. She was opposed to formal, long-
standing institutions—states, governments, big businesses,
standing armies, centralized labor unions, etc. She opposed
being controlled and manipulated. And she was fearless in
speaking her mind.

Emma Goldman Reading

I ask you . . . my friends

(you!)

you "good Americans"

you

(you!)

you "flag wavers"

you lovers of patriotism

what visions

what fantasies . . . do you cling to?

what day dreams?
What fairy tales?
Is it the old days
that you long for . . . my countrymen?
Your youths?
Your childhoods?
(The golden fields?
The rippling streams?)

Mother's Home cooking?
Grandfather's Pipe?

Apple pie?
Strolling down the lane?

Wave those banners!
Sing those songs . . . my friends!

"My eyes have seen the glory"
"O say can you see"

"Remember the Alamo!"
"Remember the Maine!"

While they smirk . . . my friends.

While they laugh . . . at you
those "bosses" . . .
(those mighty "kingpins")
. . . who own things
(and control things).

Stars . . . they feed you
(and platters of stripes).

"War!" . . . they cry.
"Beautiful, wonderful . . . glorious war!"
"Beat the drum!"
"Load the cannon!"

"Assemble!"
"March!"

"Advance!"
"Retreat!"

"Cut!"
"Shoot!"
"Bludgeon!"
"Maim!"

"Bleed my boys!"
"Sacrifice!"

While it's "Yankee Doodle" . . . that you sing
and "Over There"
("Over There!")
Your swords lifted!
Your rifles raised!

("March step!"
"Lock step!")

Blind to facts!
Blind to reality!
Like lemmings you race
(like automatons)!

It's a lie . . . my friends
(a foul deception)
these shouts
(these grand hurrahs)!

Patriotism *is* . . .
. . . the refuge of scoundrels!

They fiddle.
You dance!
They prosper.
You die!
And you never realize
(no)
who you are . . .
. . . and what you can be!

Wake up . . . good citizens!
Be not a mob . . . my friends
an "electorate"
a "body politic!"
(Be not "shepherded!")
(Be not "led!")
But be independent!
Be free!

Know your oppressor!

Fight not the "Hun" . . .
. . . nor the distant Russian
(the "Arab"

. . . not the turbaned Turk)
but the leech . . . my friends
(the war profiteer)
the corporate parasite . . . drinking your blood!

(Are you children hurting?
Are your families fed?)

Rise up . . . good people!
Rise up!

Oppose all wars
(all mass actions)

Be direct!
Be real!
Be purposeful!
Be true!

Be the hammer striking!
Be the spark intense!

Be comrades!
Be companions!
Be lovers!

Emma Goldman

Be friends!

Throw off your shackles . . . good people!
Unfetter your limbs!

The time is here!
The time is now!

Be not "buried!"
(Be not "dead!")

Resist!
(Stand tall!)

Be forceful!
Fight injustice!

The sun is shining!
Wake up!
There is a world to win!

Emma Goldman Queries

1. Is there a good kind of patriotism? Or are all forms of patriotism ultimately divisive—pitting an "us" against a "them?"

2. What do we imply when we say "our country?" Is one's country more than just a birthplace? Does "one's country" also involve a collected mythology—"the free world," "the home of the brave," "remember the Alamo," "the amber waves of grain"—a variety of preselected experiences. How is one's legacy a comfort? How a problem?

3. Is there a danger when patriotism is the *highest* value? Is there a contradiction between patriotism and Quakerism?

4. Emma Goldman sees the people as being tricked into fighting wars—as being manipulated by the powerful. Without such manipulation would ordinary people be more peace-loving, more inclined toward pacifism?

5. Emma Goldman asks her audience members to be real and true. Not to be a crowd, but a congregate of individuals. But can the people really transform society without overriding leadership—without being shepherded and led? How would a Quaker answer this question?

Dorothy Day

Dorothy Day (1897–1980), even as a small child, fell in love with Catholicism. But it was not so much the church she followed, but the simple words of Jesus, becoming a life-long advocate for the oppressed—the sick, the poor, the incarcerated and the despised. She opposed all war and violence. And it was in this spirit that she co-founded the Catholic Worker Movement.

Dorothy Day Reading: For Barbara

I was so young.
(The church . . .
. . . not even a real thing yet)
And I was in bed.
And I had . . . I think
the influenza
or the croup
(that was so prevalent).

And my father came in
and told me . . .
(so sweetly)

. . . this story
of a wicked old village woman
who was so mean
(so insufferable)
that even the devil . . . himself
despised her.
And threw her caterwauling . . .
. . . into hell.

But this same old woman . . .
(my father said)
. . . had her own special friend
(her own special guardian angel)
who loved her
(and protected her).

And so she ascended . . . then
(did this angel)
into the clouds
(into the highest heaven)
to where Jesus . . . himself
sat waiting.
(for He too . . .

my father said
. . . had always loved this woman)
And He remembered . . . now
(did Jesus)
how this same old woman
(when still a child)
had given . . . once
(to a starving beggar)
a small piece . . . of needed food.
(a shiny red carrot . . .
. . . to be precise)

And He produced . . . now
(did Jesus)
a similar . . . red carrot.

And He said . . . to the angel:
"O sweet angel!
O cherished friend!
Take now . . . this miraculous carrot.
For with it . . .
(dear helper)
. . . your special charge

might still be saved."

And so the angel . . . then
beamed . . . with pleasure.
And returned at once . . .
(my father said)
. . . to that frightful hell-hole
(to that dismal pit).
And she leaned down . . . then
(did the angel)
over its opening
over its foul . . .
. . . and glowing edge.
And she cried out . . .
(to the fallen woman):
"Listen my darling!
Listen my dear!
Grab hold . . . now
of this wondrous carrot.
And like a buried treasure . . .
. . . I will lift you up!
I will carry you to safety!"

And so she began then
(did the angel)
to raise up that woman.
To indeed lift . . .
. . . and carry her skyward.

But the other poor sinners in hell . . .
(my father said)
the other poor
(begrimed)
and battered sufferers
(the sneak-thieves
the liars
and even the vicious murderers)
(yes)
. . . they also wanted salvation
(that also wanted release).

And so they latched themselves . . . then
to the woman's two ankles
(to her firm . . .
. . . and rising legs)
and cried out . . . so sadly:

(so plaintively)
"O fortunate woman!
O compassionate friend!
We *too* . . . would rise upward!
We *too* . . . would breathe air!"

But that mean old woman . . .
(my father said)
that cruel
and pitiless creature
(yes)
. . . despised these sinners
(and cursed at them)
and kicked . . . viciously
at their hopeful fingers
(at their grasping hands)
causing them . . . then
(these sinners)
to fling out their arms
to topple backwards
(to fall).

And at that very moment
at that very instant . . . of release
(my father said)
that miraculous carrot

(that gift from Jesus)
yes
broke . . . it did
(it shattered).

And that woman . . . also
(then)
that cruel . . .
. . . and disdainful creature
(yes)
also went falling
also went plunging . . .
(backwards)
. . . into that terrible abyss.

And so the angel . . . then
flew back to Jesus.
And again . . . she pleaded her case.

But Jesus Christ . . .
(our loving savior)
. . . was also in tears.
And held . . . out to her . . .
(sweetly)
. . . His open hands
(his bleeding palms).

And He said . . . then
to the weeping angel:
"O bright . . . angel of mercy!"
O sweet . . . angel of love!
Didn't you realize . . .
(dear friend)
. . . that when she cursed those sufferers
it was me that she cursed?
And when she struck . . . at their bodies
it was mine that she hit?

For their tears . . . are my own."
(said Jesus)
"And their pain . . . rushes through me."

(and Jesus Christ . . . continued his weeping)

And I sat up in bed then.
(I remember)
And I shivered.
(and I shook)

And I cried out . . . then
to my loving father:
"I will save those sinners daddy!
I will bring them . . . carrots some day!"

And my father . . . then
(my dear sweet father)
smiled at me
(and I trembled . . . I remember)
and he bid me to sleep
(to calm myself).

But even then . . . I knew
(yes!)
(even then)
that even though I was feverish
(that even though I was young)
that I had found . . .
(somehow)
. . . my true vocation.
That I had found . . . somehow
my real life!

"O . . . those poor doomed sinners"
(I remember thinking).
"O those poor . . . miserable things!

I will listen for their voices!" . . . I cried.
I will pull them up!
I will carry them to safety!"

Dorothy Day Queries

1. Is it arrogant (or even sacrilegious) for an individual (like the little girl) to want to *personally* save the most corrupted and despised sinners? Isn't this God's job?

2. Is there a contradiction between a God of love (Jesus), and the idea of punishment (hell)?

3. In telling this story to his little girl, what moral lesson might her father have wanted to instill?

4. If your own child expressed a willingness to dedicate her entire life to those oppressed and suffering, how would you react?

5. Could such a "true vocation" (as that expressed by the little girl) find a place *within* a conventional, organized religion?

Myles Horton

Myles Horton (1905–1990) founded the Highlander Folk School in rural Tennessee in 1932 as a crucible for social action. Often ordinary people who had the means and desire for working with others were invited to attend. And through stimulating contact with teachers and each other, these students became the vital participants (and prime organizers) in the Labor and Civil Rights movements.

Myles Horton Reading: The Highlander Folk School

I thought . . . Agnes

this man was crazy!

(can you believe it!)

I really did.

I'm only . . .

(after all)

. . . just a beautician

(an ordinary hair dresser)

and a pretty good one . . . too.

And I tell you . . . my shop
(down on South Street)
is always a-buzz
"Who's doing this?"
"Who's doing that?"

It's like a town newspaper . . . almost:
("*The Daily Gossip*").

And so . . . anyway
(can you believe it?)
this man . . . comes in
(this white man . . . from Tennessee)
(this Myles Horton person).

And he says to me . . . "Bernice"
(he says to me real quiet)
"all of you Negro people
(God knows)
try to vote" . . . he says.
"But you can't pass . . .
. . . that test they give you
(that phony reading test).
What you need now" . . .

(he says)
. . . "is a way to pass that test
(a way to beat it)."

And so . . . he convinces me
(then)
(this Myles Horton)
to go back with him . . .
. . . to this little school he runs
to this Highlander Folk School
(a kind of radical
protesting place . . . he has).

And he asks me . . . immediately
(right off)
if I would like to start . . . teaching a class
a special reading class
(he says)
to help people . . . register to vote.
(me!)
(like I'm some kind of expert!)

And so then he gives me . . .
(I swear it!)

one of those little . . . classrooms
(one of those little . . . old-fashioned grade school rooms)
with blackboards
(and book shelves)
and those straight little rows they have.

And so I said . . . to him
"Listen Myles" . . . I said
"nobody I know . . .
. . . will stand for this kind of treatment.
There are serious, grown-up
adult people coming here . . . Myles
(good people . . . working people).

So let's get rid" . . .
(I said)
. . . "of these desks
and these rows of seats
and get ourselves . . . a big round table
and some real chairs
and a nice box . . . of writing supplies"
(I told him)
"and we'll go on . . .

. . . just working from there."

And honestly . . . Agnes
(I tell you)
on that first day teaching
(really)
(I swear to you)
some of those folks
some of those brand-new . . .
. . . reading students we got
(God bless them)
acted like . . .
. . . they were gonna be shot
(like they were gonna be strung up sideways).

So I said to them . . . "Listen folks
(listen" . . . I told them)
"just get easy now
(get yourselves relaxed)
and we'll write down . . .
(maybe)
some descriptions of our . . . jobs
or our gardens.

Or maybe just . . . describe
what our feet look like."

(and they all laughed at this)

And after a while . . . Agnes
(I tell you)
we were writing out . . . grocery lists
and "our true life stories"
(and things like that).

(and just getting . . .
you know
. . . to know each other pretty good).

When one day
(you know)
we were just working along
practicing our writing
(making good progress . . . I thought)
when someone noticed
(they did)
this big old . . . fancy
Declaration of Independence poster

(this poster . . .
of that famous document)
just pinned up there
just stuck on the wall.

And so we decided then . . . Agnes
(the whole bunch of us)
to take that "Declaration" . . . down
and just copy out
(line by line)
all those big fancy . . .
. . . important words it has
(you know . . . to just practice our penmanship).

And honestly . . . Agnes
(I tell you)
when we got to that . . . first
(famous)
(beginning part)
of that Declaration . . . of Independence
(that part that declares
that all men . . . are created equal)
this one big man

(this one big angry ... cotton farmer)
he stands up ... Agnes
and shouts out at me ... real loud:
"Well Miss Bernice Robinson
if we're all so damned ... exactly equal,
how come"
(he says)
"we have to sit here ... quiet
like a bunch of school children?

No white folks sitting here" ... he says
("not a single one).
They just simply *vote!*" ... he says
"they just ... *participate!*"

And then ... Agnes
(I swear)
every person
(the whole big ... class of us)
starts shouting out loud ... "That's right!
That's right Brother!
You tell it like it is ... Brother!
You tell it like it is!"

And by the time ... Agnes

we got to the last part . . . of that Declaration
(to that final part . . . that says
that *all* people . . . have the right
to protest things)

(to even throw out . . . if they want
the whole government itself).

That's when . . . I tell you
(my goodness)
it was like . . . Agnes
a great big gun going off
(a great big explosion).

And we weren't going . . .
(no)
(we decided)
. . . to be treated
(no)
like school children anymore . . . Agnes
(like frightened sheep . . .
. . . or "sweet old colored people")
but have pride . . . Agnes
(and determination)
and become a real serious

school for citizenship . . . Agnes
(a kind of citizenship center)
a place for learning things
(and changing things)
and teaching other people . . .
. . . how to change things.

And to finally start saying . . . no more of this!
No more of this trash!
No more of this dog's treatment!

No more of this feeling . . . bad all the time
and hurtful
(and hateful)

and feeble
(and broken down).

And Agnes . . . honey
(sweetie)
(I swear)
when we said these things
when we decided . . . finally
to stand our ground
good Lord . . .
(heavens!)

. . . it was like drinking air.
It was like being tossed up . . .
. . . and spread all over.

And my goodness . . . child
(I swear)
(whoooo!)
we just tore the roof . . .
. . . off that place.
We just shook the walls . . .
. . . off that old Highlander Folk School.
I swear!
I swear we did!
Indeed we absolutely . . . certainly did!

(heavens!)
(mercy!)

Agnes . . .
(child!)
(lord!)

God . . . you should have seen us darlin'!

You should have seen us . . .
(o mercy!)
. . . just flapping our wings!

Myles Horton Queries

1. Identify a time when you felt a call—when someone or something asked you to stretch—to leap into the unknown.

2. Myles Horton found that Bernice Robinson's beauty parlor was a good place to organize—a place where people naturally gathered to discuss community problems.

    If you were an organizer, where would you go to take the pulse of *your* community?

3. The reading students are being taught by a peer— by someone caught in their own social and cultural predicament.

    What are the advantages of having such an indigenous teacher? What are the drawbacks?

4. After reading the words about equality in the Declaration of Independence, both the students and their teacher seem to explode. Something is unleashed in them, and they will never be the same.

    Can you think of a similar occurrence in your own life—an epiphany? Something that put you on a new path?

5. The Highlander Folk School often taught selected people how to organize others. It was a crucible for both the Labor Movement and the Civil Rights Movement.

    Can society be transformed? Are the days of big movements over?

Fay Honey Knopp

Fay Honey Knopp (1918–1995) was a
Quaker recorded minister, a fashion
merchandiser, a singer, a writer, a peace-
activist, and a pioneer in the treatment of
sex-offenders. As a spokesperson for the
oppressed and disadvantaged, she often spoke to groups of
professionals.

Fay Honey Knopp Reading

I am so fearful
(my friends)
(my colleagues)
(in the months . . .
. . . and years to come)
if we lose our tenderness
(if we lose our love)
then merely "professionals" . . . will we be
merely "functionaries."

There is a story
(so often told)
of a team . . .

. . . of mountain climbers.
Of a group
of adventurers . . . so brave
(so intrepid)
who were climbing one day
(progressing nicely)
when one of their members
(one of their very own party)
slipped . . . he did
(stumbled)
and fell . . . helplessly
upon a jagged rock.

And as he lay there moaning . . .
(and crying)
. . . and twisting in pain
his slight gash
(his open wound)
so tiny at first
(so barely noticeable)
began swelling . . . it did
began bulging
(and pulsing)

and dripping so horribly
that his astonished comrades
(repulsed by the sight)
became sickened . . . they did
(became nauseated)
and left him . . .
(their companion)
. . . to languish there hopelessly
to suffer alone.

And O how they sped then
(these climbers).

And O how they soared!

The day brightened.
The trail shone.

Such power . . . they felt
(such splendid release).

Nothing could contain them!
The summit was theirs!

But gradually . . . my colleagues

(so very gradually)
they realized . . .
(these climbers)
. . . that alongside their comrade
(that alongside . . . their maimed
and fallen friend)
they had left their integrity.
They had left their soul.

And one of their party . . .
(then)
. . . cried out to the others:
"O tell me my comrades!
(my associates)
what has become . . .
. . . of that one who is missing?
What has become . . .
. . . of our comrade who fell?

Is he still . . .
. . . reaching out to us?
Is he still . . . calling our names?

The clouds have thickened.
(the wind increased)

Our steps seem more leaden now!
This mountain more steep!"

And so they turned . . .
(they did)
. . . away from that summit.
(away they turned . . .
. . . from that beckoning pcak)
And went back to where . . .
. . . their comrade had fallen.
Where crumpled, he lay
contorted in pain.

For the wound . . . in his side
had so terribly deepened.
And O how it festered!
O how it bled!

Their friend . . .
(they realized)
. . . was feverish now
(delirious).

His limbs twitching wildly.
His breathing in gasps.

"O let us move closer!"
(one climber cried softly).
"And furnish him comfort!"
(another proclaimed).

And so they sat . . .
(they did)
. . . with their fallen companion.
And they lifted his body . . .
. . . from that desolate ground.

And then . . . downward
they wended
(so carefully downward).

(one small step . . .
. . . following another small step)

Until one of the climbers
asked of the others:
"What has become . . .
. . . of our glorious enterprise?

What has become . . . of our mission so clear?

So intent . . . we were
on swiftly ascending
that with arrogance we climbed
(with total disdain)."

And so they led their companion . . .
. . . down those trails ever-twisting.
And they held him
(and consoled him).

And they suffered his shrieks.

And they walked all that morning . . .
. . . under cliffs over-hanging.

And in darkness they wandered
(through perilous gloom).

And they prized their companion.
(and they loved him)

And they huddled around him.

And they kept him from cold.

Fay Honey Knopp Queries

1. Are external goals (e.g., climbing a mountain) merely superficial? Should one concentrate instead on inner, more spiritual accomplishments?

2. Can societal advancement ever be reconciled with a concern for the less fortunate?

3. Why do the mountain climbers give up on their goal? Are they just feeling guilty? What can giving up possibly gain?

4. Why do the mountain climbers come to love and prize their companion?

5. What would lead the speaker to relate this story to her colleagues—a group of budding professionals? Is there something wrong with professionalism? Must profession-alism lead to arrogance?

Dr. Martin Luther King, Jr.

 Dr. Martin Luther King, Jr. (1929–1968) was a leading voice of the Civil Rights Movement in the United States. He was a teacher of nonviolence, a student of Jesus, Gandhi and Thoreau and a practitioner of civil disobedience. At the time of his assassination he was planning a march against economic injustice. In hundreds of sermons and speeches he spoke out for the end of segregation and the healing of racial wounds.

Dr. Martin Luther King, Jr. Reading

It's hard . . . my friends
(so hard!)
(so very hard!)
to understand these words.

(O Heavens it's hard!)

To hear again
and still again:
"Be sweet . . . you suffering Negroes!"
"Be realistic!"

"Resign yourselves!"
"Be meek like baby Jesus!"

(so hard)
(so very hard it is!)

And even our own good ministers
(o yes!)
even our very own Negro ministers . . .
(praise Jesus!)
. . . cry out to us:
"Be calm you restless Negroes!
Be patient!
For Rome wasn't built in a day!"
(O no!)

(so hard it is!)
(so very hard it is!)

Well we *have* been patient . . . my friends!
(that's right!)
And we have been calm.
And we have been . . . peaceful
and prayerful
and obedient . . .

(praise Jesus!)
. . . to the law of the land!

(that's right . . . that's certainly right!)

But our dear Negro children . . .
(O mercy!)
. . . still cry in the night-time.
And our poor Negro husbands . . .
. . . still lower their eyes.
(God bless them!)

And our fine Negro women
(Good glory!)
our fine excellent . . . Negro women
(that's right!)
still labor my friends
still toil . . . like the Israelites
in the white folks' homes.

(how hard it is!)
(how very hard it is!)

(O . . . how hard it is!)
(how very hard it is!)

But these years of suffering . . . I tell you
are fast concluding
And these days of abasement . . .
. . . are nearing their end.

For no more injustice . . .
. . . shall we tolerate!
(no sir!)
And no more humiliation . . . shall we stand!

For we are gathered this morning
with affection . . . dear people
We are gathered together . . .
(oh yes!)
. . . in sweetness
and purpose
and great joyful release.
For we are free in the Lord!
(Praise Jesus!)
We are free . . .
(O God Almighty!)
. . . in our great and glorious Lord!
(that's right!)

So you can batter our bodies . . . Mr. Klansman!
(okay!)
And you can burn down our schoolrooms . . . Mr. Night
Rider!
And you can holler!
And you can yell!
And you can shout out:
"Get up from that bus seat . . . Mr. Negro!"
(that's right!)
Get up from that all-white . . . Woolworth's lunch
counter!"
(get up!)
(get yourselves up!)

But you can't crush our spirits . . . Mr. Sheriff!
(O no!)
And you can't crack our souls . . . Mr. Policeman!
(no way!)
For like that tree
(that tree!)
that's standing by the water
we shall . . .
(no!)

. . . we shall not be moved!
(that bright and beautiful tree!)

(O Lord!)
(My bountiful Lord!)

O Lord!
My bountiful Lord!

So bring on your police dogs . . . Bull Connor!
(yes sir!)
And your billy clubs . . . Chief Pritchett!
And your cattle prods!
And your fire hoses!
And send . . . even
(yes!)
our small children to jail
our small . . . lovely little children!

And you can chain down their bodies!
(Chief Pritchett!)
And bind up their ankles
(Bull Connor!)
And songs of freedom . . . will they sing!
And songs of love!
And songs of sweet and tender forgiveness!

(that's right!)
(that's certainly right!)

And so we ask you now . . . dear people
we ask you *right* now
(O yes!)
if you love freedom
to stand here with us . . . good people!

If you love America . . . to stand here with us!

Black folks . . . if you love freedom
(stand here with us!)

White folks . . . if you love freedom
(stand here with us!)

Rabbis and priests
(stand here with us!)

Both rich man and poor man
(stand here with us!)

The crowds in the cities
(stand here with us!)
. . . and the folks in the towns
(stand here with us!)

Dr. Martin Luther King, Jr.

From the North to the South . . . and the East to the West
if you love freedom
(if you love justice)
stand here with us!
(stand here with us!)

And those with compassion . . . stand here with us!

For the day is coming . . . dear people
(O yes!)
That great day
(that glorious day!)
when the lion *will* . . .
. . . lie down with the lamb!
And the white folks *will* . . .
. . . sit down with the black folks
and the brown folks
and the red folks . . . and the yellow folks!
And everyone *will* . . .
(O Glory!)
. . . sit themselves down!

For we are all one people!
(Praise Jesus!)
We are all one dear . . . indivisible people

(that's right!)
(that's certainly right!)

•   •   •

What a great day
(O yes!)
to be walking toward freedom . . . good people!
What a great day . . .
(O Glory!)
. . . to be marching toward light!

What a good day!

What a perfect day!

What a good and great and beautiful day!

(you tell it brother!)
(you tell it straight!)

(you sing it!)
(you shout it out!)

(A-men brother!)
(A-men!)

Dr. Martin Luther King, Jr. Queries

1. Why would the more conventional Negro ministers, in the face of abuse, urge their congregations to be "sweet," "calm," "realist" and "patient?" In other words, to "turn the other cheek?"

2. Dr. King tells his listeners that though enslaved, they are "free in the Lord." And that this freedom will give them the strength to stand for their rights: "For like that tree standing by the water, we shall not be moved."

   How does this idea of passive resistance differ from turning the other cheek?

3. Dr. King is willing to let even small children demonstrate—to put their bodies on the line and even risk jail.

   Can this treatment of children be justified?

4. Is Dr. King's call to have protesters "passively" accept punishment (to nonviolently resist) too much to ask of most people? What possible effect could this action have on the powerful?

5. Have times changed? Have people changed? Could this strategy of passive nonviolent resistance work today? And is passive resistance simply a strategy —a tactic?

6. In asking for all types of people to come together (regardless of race, class, ethnicity, etc.) Dr. King employs a preaching style—he delivers a sermon.

   Is his style too narrow? Would many outside of King's Christian tradition be turned off?

   If he had lived, could Dr. King have led a truly *national* movement?

Juanita Nelson

Juanita Nelson (1923–) has had a long
career grounded in non-violence, and
under this discipline has functioned as a
tax-resistor, a peace activist and a fighter
for integration. Her basic strategy has been non-coopera-
tion. She will not allow the government (or any authority)
to tell her what to do—especially if it means desecrating the
rights and lives of others. Her answer to coercion has often
been the hunger strike and the jail sentence.

Juanita Nelson Reading

I tell you it was . . . like
one of those cops and robbers movies
(sweetie).
One of those funny . . . ones
where the police start banging
on your bedroom door.

And there I was
half-awake
(practically bare-naked)
trying to get . . .
. . . my bathrobe fastened.

When in . . .
. . . they came anyway
(I swear it!)
these two . . . humongous
"tax cops"

"Internal Revenue agents" . . .
. . . they called themselves.

(one of them . . . at least
nine feet tall)

informing me . . . that I
(Juanita Nelson)
owed the U.S. government . . . exactly
nine hundred
and fifty-nine dollars
(and eighty-three cents).

And they were intending . . . now
(they said)
to drag my poor . . . black
(and bath-robed body)
to the local hoosegow.

(a place . . . not exactly
unknown to me)

But I decided then
honey
(I really did)
that since these taxes . . . go
for the making of weapons
(for the killing . . . of poor
and innocent people)

that I was not . . . about
(in no way!)
to help them out.

So I plunked myself . . . down
(sweetheart)
like a stone
(like a sack . . .
. . . of wet cement).

And O
how they cursed me, sweetie.
O . . .

. . . how they grabbed at my arms
(and my legs).
All the while . . . calling out
for more cops
(more reinforcements).

And soon darling
(I tell you)
every fool . . . policeman
in captivity
was pulling me
(and tugging me).
And dragging me out
(finally)
to this big . . . old
paddy wagon car
they had waiting.

(the wind blowing)

(my poor old . . . bathrobe
flapping in the breeze)

And honey I just *knew*

that *they* knew
all about my political past
(all about my . . . "subversive"
and "agitating" ways).

And darling I *was* scared.

And I thought about . . . Gandhi
(and Thoreau)
and what . . . Sojourner Truth
had to go through.

And I had to laugh, honey
(I had to cry).
For here I was
"me!"
("the great Juanita Nelson")
a tiny black . . .
incarcerated
. . . "tax resistor"
(a kind of fool)
(a kind of scarecrow)

owing the government

the price . . .
(perhaps)
. . . of a few old hand guns.
So what did it matter
(really)
if I paid my taxes
or didn't pay my taxes?

The wars would continue.

The killing would go on.

But I couldn't do it, honey.
(I just . . . couldn't)
I couldn't capitulate.
I just . . . couldn't
pay those taxes
(that blood money).

I'd rather . . .
. . . be a laughingstock.
I'd rather . . .
stay rotting in jail.

There was . . . just
no choice
(no alternative, darling).

It was stupid . . . I know
(I can't explain it)
but I had to be *good*

(I had to be worthy)

I had to be *true* . . .
. . . to my deepest heart.
(I just had to!)

There is so much
"awfulness" in the world.
so much "hatefulness."

(so much deceit)

And I won't
(no I won't!)
no!
(I swear it!)
. . . be a part of it.

Juanita Nelson Queries

1. What *is* the point of a single, almost *unseen*, protest—especially if it involves great hardship and inconvenience (e.g., tax resistance)?

2. Do you ever have a sense of futility about your own political activism? How does one keep protesting injustices that seem impervious to change?

3. Juanita Nelson's witness seems *not* to have the backing of a great religious belief or social philosophy (e.g., Christianity or Marxism).

   Are vague personal feelings about being good and worthy and true really enough?

4. Could you ever (as does Juanita Nelson) think of yourself as a fool? And must "fool" always be a derogatory term? What can the term "holy fool" possibly mean?

5. Is the power (and triumph) of mass culture (rapidly becoming mass global culture) making individual protest obsolete?

Ed Nagel

The Free School movement, which flourished in the 1960s and 70s was greatly influenced by A. S. Neill's Summerhill School in England and by U.S. writers and educators such as John Holt, Paul Goodman, Ed Nagel and many others.

Ed Nagel (1941–) was one of the founders of the Santa Fe Community School where students (no matter what age) were encouraged to help fashion their own rules and curriculum. Democracy was to be lived and not just understood.

Ed Nagel Reading: The Santa Fe Community School

It was kind of funny
(I remember)
because it wasn't like . . .
. . . a regular school should be.
(it was really weird)

And then Bill Hanson

(this teacher guy)
asked all of us . . . he did
what we'd like to study here.

(as if we really knew)

And then someone yelled . . . "Let's study the planets!"
And someone else yelled . . . "Let's study your butt!"

And then Alice Jean
(Carl's sister)
stood up . . . and said to us all:
"Hey everybody
(listen up now!)
Terry Cole
(that little bedbug)
has been kicking me . . . hard
on my ankle here
(that stupid jerk)
kicking me . . .
. . . and calling me *retard*."

(and she showed us . . . then
this mark that she had)

And then Terry Cole . . . jumped up
(and yelled out real loud):
"Cry baby . . . cry baby
stick your head in bean gravy!
Your breath smells . . .
. . . like a rotten garbage pail
(ha!)."

And Bill Hanson
(our main teacher)
("Big Bill")
stood up real fast . . . and said to us:
"Well my students
(since this school . . . is really *your* school)
what now
(my children)
are we going to do . . . about this thing?"

(as if we knew)

And then Terry Cole . . .
(who has rocks for brains)
. . . yelled out loud:

"Screw you!
Screw you Bill Hanson!
I hope you fall . . .
. . . in some dirty ditch water
(ha!)."

And Pat Kinney said
(then)
that Terry Cole
(yes)
should be kicked out of school . . . "like a shot"
and kicked . . . hard
on "his own dumb ankle."
(and we all cried out: "Let's kick Terry! . . . Let's kick Terry!")

And then Bill Hanson said to us:
"OK my children
(have it your own way)
but who first . . .
(now)
wants to start this righteous kicking?"

And then Terry Cole
(that ninny)

gave us the horse-laugh
(and the old stiff-finger . . . he did)
but started . . . then
(for some reason)
(I swear it's true)
to spit . . . then
all over himself
and bite down hard
on the skin of his arm.

Until Bill Hanson
(who is really . . . very strange)
took a-hold of Terry's shoulders
and started pressing them
(and squeezing them)
really, really hard.

And Alice Jean
(I swear it)
jumped to her feet
(and shouted out at Bill Hanson):
"Don't hurt him Bill!
(don't hurt him)

there's something really . . . really
wrong with Terry!"

(and Terry Cole . . . just kept wriggling
and kicking his legs out)

And Pat Kinney shouted then
that yes
(yes)
(absolutely)
we should be
(yes)
punishing Terry Cole
(really!)
but maybe . . . just
(perhaps)
by making him sit.

And we all agreed then
(yes)
that Terry Cole *could* stay
if he would first . . . sit down.

And then little Paulie

(little Paulie Morris)
(the youngest kid)
got up . . .
. . . and said to the whole classroom
that Terry Cole
seemed to him
(to be)
very, very . . . very unhappy
and needed
(he said)
a nice new . . . house to live in
("a really special house").

And so he drew for Terry
(then)
this great big fancy
millionaire's mansion . . . with a swimming pool
(and a giant swing set).

And someone said . . . "I'll draw Terry a lamp!"
And someone else said . . . "I'll draw him a row boat and a car!"
And then some servants were drawn
(and a yellow golf cart)

and a cat someone made
(and a crooked dog house)
(and a TV)
and a TV antenna also
(which Terry . . . stuck)
on top of his head
(man!).

(and we all laughed together)

And we studied then . . .
(after that)
the planets
(and the Milky Way).

And Bill told us . . .
. . . about the "constellations"
(about the "archer"
and the "twins"
and the "big and little dipper").

And then we went running outside . . .
. . . and ate sandwiches

(and sat on the ground)
and learned about the wild flowers
(and the tree names).

And Terry Cole . . .
(would you believe it)
. . . went walking with Alice Jean.

And we yelled out . . . "Lovers! . . . Lovers!"
(at them).

("Alice Jean and Terry Cole *love!*")

(and they stuck out their tongues at us)

(and we shouted "dumb" to them)
(and then we had "clean-up time")
(and then we got to go home)

And it was a pretty good day . . .
(I thought)
(sort of)
. . . if you have to go to school.

Ed Nagel Queries

1. If you were the teacher in this situation, how would you have responded to the chant of "Let's kick Terry!"?

2. In a "free school" the curriculum was very responsive to individual interests and unexpected events. There was no straight line to learning. Students could choose *not* to attend class.

   Would you enroll your child in such a school?

3. When the teacher (Bill Hanson) asked the class, "But who first wants to start this righteous kicking?" did he go too far? Was he teaching that violence could be an acceptable solution?

4. On this school day, what were the children taught? What did they learn?

5. Will a free, unprogrammed situation generally bring out the best in people? Or is a lack of overall direction an invitation to disaster?

6. Do such small experimental schools have a place in today's society? Or are they just a charming anachronism?